MW01101872

I offer this artwork to you as a mirror.
May each painting reveal both an intimate reflection
of an archetypical epiphany.
I pray that within these visions you might witness
your own sacred heart, & through this recognition
remember the divinity that dwells within.

♡
Autumn Skye

ART & SOUL

PAINTINGS BY AUTUMN SKYE

Photo by Sydney Woodward

Art is simultaneously trivial and essential. A painting is simply just colourful mud smeared on fabric, pretty and frivolous for our amusement. Paradoxically, art also has the potential to move mountains. Art can heal emotional trauma, cure illness, bring renewed vitality, and cultivate joy. It can awaken and empower both the artist and viewer, connecting straight to the emotional subconscious. It can shine light on critical issues and be a grounding touchstone of beauty in an otherwise bleak landscape. It can start revolutions, shift paradigms, and present paths forward toward wholeness.

Throughout history, society has looked to the arts to guide and inspire our personal and cultural narratives. Now, while the world is at the precipice of monumental change, artworks can be maps to help usher humanity forward into positive ways of seeing and being.

At moments of reckoning, I believe more than ever in the importance of art. In my bones dwells a sacred duty to play my small part in this collective awakening. Art propels me out of bed in the morning, whispering me awake with purpose. Since my earliest memories, I have felt a creative fire in my belly and an unyielding mission to share inspiration with the world. By learning to listen, I have come to trust the mysterious compass of the heart to navigate both my imagination and my life. I am continually humbled and empowered by the potent teachings of the visionary process.

For your journey, I offer this artwork ~ a gift from spirit, through my heart and hands, to you. May these reflections inspire your own inner knowing, authentic creativity, and resilient spirit.

DUST
TO
STARDUST

I remember that I am a facet of divinity.

I nurture this body as a temporary vessel for my eternal spirit.

I savour this moment as a miraculous gift from the generosity of life.

My heart beats faithfully while the warm earth rises to meet my feet.

I am here to live and to love and remind others that they, too, are divine.

SOPHIA'S GIFT (DETAIL)

HEALING
36"x24" acrylic on canvas, 2013

"The most beautiful thing we can experience
is the mysterious.

It is the source of all true art and science."

— ALBERT EINSTEIN

RAPTURE
12"x36" acrylic & gold leaf on canvas, 2017

*In our human yearning for meaning,
we have invented language in an attempt to
bring the vastness of reality and imagination into
our intellectual understanding.
We have shaped our words into significance,
aiming to comprehend and convey the great mystery.
We have placed immense gravity upon these terms,
and have come to insist that they themselves are sacred.*

*"Love" is just a word, and even "God" is just a word.
God: influential and inflammatory, hallowed, beautiful,
terrifying, ambiguous, and innately personal
to each soul who utters it.*

*Perhaps the word itself is a superficial label that we
have attached to the unfathomable.
Yet, a feeling is experienced when the sun shines
through the clouds and shimmers on the water's surface.
There is a wonderment that fills us when witnessing
a flock of songbirds pulsing with life while flying in unison.
There is an emotion that makes our heart leap with epiphany
and recognition when listening to a great piece of music.
There is a welling of belonging when we look into
the eyes of a loved one.
This is divinity experienced and embodied.
This is God.
These feelings of love and euphoria, life and wonder.
This is God.
Perhaps God's true name cannot be spoken,
for there is no word to accurately communicate the infinite.
Perhaps God can only be felt by the heart.*

DIVINE INTERVENTION
12"x36" acrylic on canvas, 2014

SOPHIA'S GIFT
19"x21" acrylic on canvas, 2020

REMEMBERING ETERNITY
30"x36" acrylic on canvas, 2010

FRUITION
24"x48" acrylic on canvas, 2015

In honour of the ancestors
May they anchor us to the earth
May they forgive our blunders and may their
wounds be made right by our healing

In honour of each generation
May the unique wisdom they carry
illuminate a new path and guide us towards wholeness
May our inner child, parent, and elder exist in balance

In honour of the lifetimes that we walked
before and the lifetimes that will echo on
May we continue to grow and evolve
May we seek light and be light

In honour of the Past, the Present, and the Future
May we breathe into each moment,
knowing there is only now.

WISDOM OF THE AGES
26"x40" acrylic on canvas, 2012

LIGHT WORK
61"x38" acrylic on canvas, 2016

"Once we overcome the fear of being tiny,
we find ourselves on the threshold of
a vast and awesome universe ..."

— CARL SAGAN

ORIGINS
24"x30" oil on canvas, 2023

(opposite)
DUST TO STARDUST
23.5"x31.5" acrylic & gold leaf on panel, 2020

When we stand at the threshold
of the mystery, we come face to
face with the divine cycle of birth,
life, death, and the eternal dance
of spirit. We have an opportunity
to forgive and make peace with
our shadows so that they may
be brought into the light for
transformation and healing.
Thus, we pay homage to the
ancestors and liberate
generations to come.

ESPÍRITU
12"x24" acrylic on canvas, 2016

THE
BELOVED
WITHIN

I am resilient in my centre,
balanced in the delicate dance of harmony.
I am rooted in equanimity, remaining humble
and curious amidst division and polarity.
I am grounded in my breath,
my heartbeat, and my humanity.

I am patient.
I am present.
I am peaceful.
I am love.

TAṆHĀ ~ THE DANCE OF LONGING (DETAIL)

True North is the internal
guide that navigates
us through life. It is our
constant and steady bearing,
the fixed point
in a turbulent world.
It is always available
to us when we can calm
our minds and reconnect
to our intuition.
True North is the
compass of the heart.

TRUE NORTH
40"x30" acrylic & gold leaf on canvas, 2018

TAṆHĀ ~ THE DANCE OF LONGING
23.5"x31.5" acrylic on panel, 2018

PHOENIX RISING
24"x36" acrylic & gold leaf on canvas, 2019

Your beating heart, honesty, and courageous humanity are gifts to the world.
Embody your strength and tenderness.
Walk softly, and yet keep your power.
Roar your truth, share your love, and stay strong.

STAY STRONG
30"x40" acrylic on canvas, 2021

These are extreme and polarizing times.
May we dwell in the middle way, the nexus point of delicate balance.
Even as the world around us erupts into furor and confusion,
we can allow our tears and laughter without attachment.
We can remain at peace in our innermost centre and be a witness to it all.

MIDDLE WAY
36"x 48" acrylic on canvas, 2020

I am a manifestation of love, a unique facet of the universe, a sacred spark of creation's fire.
I remember my divinity and am coming home to the sanctum of my indwelling spirit.
I live with integrity, passion, and humility.
My heart is my guide towards truth.

"The Kingdom of God is within you." — LUKE 17:21

DIVINE HUMANITY
24"x36" acrylic on canvas, 2021

The Sacred Mother is awakening within me, and I am reclaiming my vitality.
The Divine Lover is awakening within me, and I embrace my sensuality.
The Holy Queen is awakening within me, and I am stepping into my sovereignty.
I am cultivating my intuition and empowering my innate wisdom.
I am on the path of Love.
I am whole.
I am holy.

HOLY GRAIL
24"x36" acrylic on canvas, 2020

When we dream, there are no borders or limits.
The division between you and me dissolves, and all that remains
is boundless possibility.

When we dream, we communicate in symbols.
Our breath moves in rhythm with lullabies,
our eyelids weighted with stories of yesterday and tomorrow.

When we dream, the edges of the real and imagined blur,
and we swim in the inky pools of distorted memories.

When we dream, we are explorers and warriors, dancers and flyers.
When we dream, we are together...

(opposite)

THE VITALITY OF TOUCH
10"x8" acrylic on panel, 2020

SHARED LULLABY
8"x10" acrylic on panel, 2020

This is a mirror to your innate strength, compassion, and grace.
It is a mirror to the community that stands with you and around you,
always and forever in the spiritual and ancestral realms.
You are not alone.
You belong.

"Communication is merely an exchange of information,
but connection is an exchange of our humanity."

— SEAN STEPHENSON

ATMA - THE GUIDE OF SOULS
24"x36" acrylic on canvas, 2022

It's ok to care deeply,
yet don't let sorrow dampen your gratitude
or distract you from savouring life's small joys.
It's ok to mourn what is lost,
yet don't let the inertia and weight of despair
rob you of the gifts of grief and healing.
It's ok to feel fully,
and to soften into the movement of emotion and sensation,
yet do not be disoriented in the wilderness of reactions.
Keep your footing grounded
and hold your gaze to the horizon of hope.
It's ok to take space for rest,
yet don't let apathy subdue your creative impulse
or smother your motivation to seek solutions.
Your body is your temple.
Go within.
Lay your burden upon the altar of your indwelling spirit,
your heart an offering in service to love.
Look back for wisdom,
look forward for hope,
and stay present to embody peace.

MY BODY, MY TEMPLE
51"x67" acrylic on linen, 2015

ANIMAL SPIRIT

I am a part of nature, not apart from it.
The microcosm of my body and spirit
are aligning in right relationship with
the macrocosm of the earth.
I am harmonizing with the hum of creation.
I honour all of existence; every creature that
flies or swims, slithers or walks the earth.
I celebrate the miraculous tapestry of life
that makes up this diverse animal
family of which I am one.

THE FELLOWSHIP (DETAIL)

DAYBREAK
48"x24" acrylic on canvas, 2020

48

48

"The imagination is the golden
pathway to everywhere."

— TERENCE MCKENNA

Unlock that within you
which longs to soar.
Be brave, dear heart, open and let go.
Allow your spirit to be stirred
by the rustle of feathers
and the beating of wings.
Let the wind lift you, and surrender
to the boundless sky's embrace.
You are safe, and you are free
to live with wild abandon.

"Life is a balance between
holding on and letting go."

— RUMI

WILD ABANDON
24"x30" acrylic on canvas, 2019

FREEDOM CRY
36"x30" acrylic on canvas, 2017

"Never explain, never retract, never apologize,
just get the thing done and let them howl!"

— NELLIE MCCLUNG

TWILIGHT VIGIL
8"x10" oil on panel, 2022

(opposite)

LUCID VISION
26"x40" acrylic on canvas, 2009

Remember, there is truth and
illusion in everything witnessed.
Our perception is a tool
of manifestation, whether
conscious or not.
Creative energy is imbued
wherever we focus,
so we must wisely choose
how to direct the power
of our attention.
Concepts become form;
form inevitably dissolves
into memory, and memory
circles back into imagination.
In such an ambiguous reality,
we must stay curious
and objective.
If we hold our convictions
lightly and embrace our
childlike wonder,
we may yet remember
how to fly!

PERCEPTION
20"x16" acrylic on canvas, 2021

THE FREQUENCY OF SWEETNESS
14"x12" acrylic on panel, 2023

(opposite)

PURA VIDA
24"x36" acrylic on canvas, 2013

Autumn Leyet 2013

HOPE
35"x40" acrylic on canvas, 2018-2021

"Be soft. Do not let the world make you hard.
Do not let the pain make you hate.
Do not let the bitterness steal your sweetness.
Take pride that even though the rest of the world may disagree,
you still believe it to be a beautiful place."

— IAIN THOMAS

WHALE SONG
18"x72" acrylic on canvas, 2015

Identify what intimidates you and lean in.
Look it in the eye, show your vulnerability, and bare your heart.
Every step you take towards your highest potential will be matched by resistance,
so expect the fear to come.
We get comfortable with living small and limiting our dreams.
We make excuses for why we cannot grow or change.
We allow judgement, comparison, and perfectionism to feed the inertia,
keeping us stuck in old patterns.
So find the resistance, name the monster, and make friends with your fear.

KIN
20"x16" acrylic on canvas, 2020

PROVIDENCE
18"x72" acrylic & gold leaf on canvas, 2018

THE MAIDEN'S COURAGE
40"x30" acrylic on canvas, 2023

THE WITNESS
20"x16" acrylic on canvas, 2023

(opposite)
THE ALLURE
16"x20" acrylic on canvas, 2023

THE PACT
26"x30" acrylic on canvas, 2016

Beloved friend,
you are not alone.
You are loved,
you are valid,
and you are vital
to the whole.
Beloved friend,
we are stronger together.
We are worthy of
each other's time
and affection and are
growing and
healing in tandem.
Beloved friend,
thank you for teaching me.
Thank you for
witnessing my humanity.
Beloved friend,
I am here still holding
your hand.
Our lives are braided
together no
matter the minutes,
months, or miles
between us.
Beloved friend,
you are the mirror
to my light and shadow,
and I am boundlessly grateful
for all that you are.

AMAZING GRACE
24"x48" acrylic &
gold leaf on canvas, 2018

Reclaim the sacredness of life and inhabit your
unique presence within this time and space.

Each conscious breath and each soul-charged
heartbeat blesses the temple of your body.

Come home to the sanctum of your indwelling spirit.

EMBODIMENT
23.5"x31.5" acrylic on panel, 2018

Each creature that crosses our path is a reflection of
aspects of ourselves; our body, heart, mind, and spirit.

This painted mirror offers four animals to represent these facets:

The snake reminds us of the rich depth and healing available
when we traverse the underworld and face our shadow.
It also encourages our discernment to choose somatically
what is and is not for our highest good.

The lion is grounded in heart and courage. It invokes our
fierce compassion, the brave warrior within,
and the integrity at our core.

The owl invites our wonder and connection to spirit.
It inspires our curiosity and ignites our innate wisdom.

The butterfly dwells in the between worlds,
the liminal space of transformation.
It tenderly alights on the mind's eye as a guide for intuition.

They are us, and we are them.
We are a part of nature, not apart from it.

STEWARDS OF THE MYSTIC
16"x20" oil on canvas, 2022

THE FELLOWSHIP
36"x18" acrylic on canvas, 2023

SENTINEL
20"x16" acrylic & gold leaf on canvas, 2023

(opposite)
ASTRAL PLAINS
20"x16" acrylic on canvas, 2023

SONG OF THE MAKERS
60"x30" acrylic on canvas, 2023

If we get silent enough and open our hearts to wonder,
we can hear the Song of the Makers amongst the stars of the night sky.
This is the music of the primordial ones, timeless and vast,
the ageless titans in a ceaseless odyssey of the void.
In their wake floats creation, new galaxies and worlds birthed from
their singing, effervescent and full of potential.

MIRRORS

I am curious and compassionate.
I ignite the torch of awareness,
illuminating the dark corners of my unconscious.
I am humble and patient in the process
of deepening and expanding.
I honour my unique journey of growth.
I live in gratitude for the miracle of life.

SWEET TABOO (DETAIL)

(opposite)

INDIGO
16"x20" acrylic & gold leaf on canvas, 2018

SWEET TABOO
16"x20" acrylic on canvas, 2022

The land is reawakening with the swelling of tree buds and the climbing of the sun. Green saturates grey, and levity tickles at the corners of The Green Man's eyes.

He heralds a sweet relief of burgeoning hope after a dark season. The composting stories of yesterday nourish the fruit of tomorrow, his promise of sweetness.

He is the steadfast and faithful masculine who guards the endless cycles of birth, life, death, and rebirth. While aged and wise, he exudes a playful sensuality and a mischievous lightheartedness.

He tends to the wild and fertile feminine, and together they dance to an eternal rhythm of decay and unfolding.

"God of wilderness, God of wildness,
lead me to the quiet places of my soul.
In stillness, in openness, may I find my strength."

— JAN L. RICHARDSON

TENDER OF THE WILD
16"x20" acrylic on canvas, 2022

HONEY
16"x20" acrylic on canvas, 2017

SOUL RETRIEVED
16"x20" acrylic on canvas, 2018

To the terrestrial and the celestial, the internal and external,
the complexity of soil and the simplicity of stars.
To the deep inward nexus of manifestation,
and the infinite vastness reaching out beyond comprehension.
To the tapestry of life, the eternally woven threads of mycelium and magic.
To the light, the dark, and the intricate communion of creation and decay.

THE GENEROUS QUEEN
30"x40" acrylic on canvas, 2024

WHITE HART
16"x20" acrylic on canvas, 2017

(opposite)

THE GIFT OF THE MAGI
16"x20" acrylic, frankincense, myrrh, & 24k gold leaf on canvas, 2018

She circles the earth in time with
the ceaselessly breaking twilight
of the new day.
Bearing witness to the light,
she whispers awake
a slumbering world.
Her gaze remains ever focused
on the horizon and the expansive
thread of possibilities.
Along the way, she tucks trinkets
and stories into the folds
of her cloak,
treasures to remind her of the magic
within each ephemeral moment.

DAWN'S WITNESS
20"x16" acrylic on canvas, 2019

THE
JOURNEY
HOME

I trust in the journey.
I envision a benevolent future.
I savour the richness of each moment.
I am held even in my pain.
I believe in love.

MYCELIUM DREAMING (DETAIL)

"Do not feel lonely,
the entire universe
is inside you."

— RUMI

VIRTUAL/REALITY
60"x40" acrylic on canvas, 2015

LIBERTY
14"x42" acrylic on canvas, 2016

The storm of our mind, our life, and the world around us can seem tumultuous, at times truly terrifying
with waves of intensity and raw force. It may bring up fears, or trigger our fight or flight instincts.
It can shake us to our foundation, tormenting us to surrender to the chaos. However, if we can remember
our heart centre, quiet our mind, and come back to our breath, we can claim inner calm.
As a witness to the furor, our compassion becomes a beacon of light in the raging storm.

TRUE HARBOUR
48"x48" acrylic on canvas, 2017

(opposite) MOURNING DUE
30"x42" acrylic on canvas, 2015

PIETA
48"x56" acrylic on canvas, 2016

ETERNAL WATERS
48"x24" acrylic on canvas, 2018

In honour of the sacred and life-giving water that flows through us and all things.
This water is more ancient than the earth itself and will never cease to be. The same drop of water that fell
in an Indian monsoon, flowed down the Amazon, and was sipped in a fine cup of tea in China.
It floated in mist over the Orkney Isles, was distilled into tinctures by ancient medicine makers, and crashed
in thunderous waves against the shores of Hawaii. It has moistened a tissue to clean a child's face, swirled in
snowstorms over mountaintops, dripped from branches onto mossy forest floors, then mixed with pigments for
masterpieces of art. This is the same water that flows from our eyes in a moment of pure emotion. Like the spark of our spirit,
water is eternal, only changing shape and expression as it journeys through existence in a timeless dance.

We are healing the lineage of our fathers.

Generation upon generation of boys learning early to stifle their tears
and to calcify their tenderness. Each child challenged to be the
toughest in the crowd, hide his heart, and go to battle.

This inherited weight is normalized and internalized. Unaware of the
tools of communication, compassion, and vulnerability that could elevate
his unspeakable burden, he swallows his words and puts on a brave face.

The grief is buried, and stoically, each follows in his father's footsteps,
believing that silence or rage are signs of strength.
He teaches his sons to do the same.

Wars are waged, conquest mistaken for love, the feminine oppressed,
the natural world dominated...

And here we stand now in a vast landscape of stone,
each tender warrior straining under generations of story and antiquity.

This is the work before us in this life: to stand in our strength and be brave;
then soften, listen, and open.

This is the work that will help repair the fissures in the tapestry
of humanity and the world.

We are healing the lineage of our fathers' fathers, and in doing so we
are healing that of our sons' sons.

OUR FATHERS' SONS
24"x48" acrylic on canvas, 2022

Slow down

Slow down

Slow down

Get quiet

Be patient

Listen

Remember
what is truly important

Remember
who you are

Remember
you belong to the earth.

MYCELIUM DREAMING
48"x38" acrylic on canvas, 2018

"Your commitment to your wellness
is part of the revolution."

— Danielle LaPorte

SHELTER FOR OPENING
48"x36" acrylic & found objects on canvas, 2009

REGENERATION
18"x24" acrylic on panel, 2013

THE CALL OF THE RIVER
30"x40" acrylic on canvas, 2013

We are all searching for home, the land from which our bones were born.

We long for belonging. To know a place deeply in our our feet and fingertips, to feel our heartbeat and tears one with the stones and rivers.

We are orphans, you see, displaced cultures and spirit. Our lineage lost, abandoned, stolen, hidden. Along the way we forgot the path home. We had to, it was a matter of survival. We had to begin anew, carve a hopeful future and liberate our stories from the weight of the past. Our allegories and songs faded from our lips, our rituals and customs buried under layers of shame and fear, our heirlooms burned.

We do not even recognize our own reflection in the lakes anymore, we no longer hear our grandmother's voice in the wind.

How can we feel at home when we've forgotten what home feels like?

However, perhaps if we just stop running for a moment, take off our shoes and dig our toes into the dirt, we might begin to remember. If we can pause and take a deep breath, feel the sun on our face and wind in our hair, we might hear the distant echoing of familiar songs and laughter. If we can just quiet our striving and lay our body on the land, we might notice our heartbeat slow and sync with the rhythm of the earth, and the blood in our veins weave in tune with the flowing water beneath the ground.

For what has been forgotten is not really gone. Though we have travelled far, we have not actually left home behind.

The more miles I walk, the more I realize that home is under my feet and always has been. My roots remain tethered and true. I belong here, wherever I might place my next footstep. If I pay attention, I can notice the earth rise subtly up to meet my touch, welcoming me home. And, in turn, I can offer gratitude, and allow myself to sink a little deeper into her embrace.
"Thank you Grandmother. I am here. I love you. Please forgive my forgetfulness. I remember now. With you, I belong."

ANCIENT ONES
30"x40" acrylic on canvas, 2018

Growth is inevitable, change is imminent, and the compost of yesterday will nourish the fruit of tomorrow.

(opposite)
PLENTY
30"x40" acrylic on canvas, 2018

SOLACE
36"x24" acrylic on canvas, 2020

Autumn Skye 2020

THE LANGUAGE OF STILLNESS
36"x18" acrylic & gold leaf on canvas, 2023

"Science is just measured magic,
therefore magic is science that is yet to be understood."

— NEO ALEXANDER CORBETT

ALCHEMY

I am made of infinite ingredients,
light and dark, spirit, bones, and stardust.
I am a thread woven into the song of creation.
I stand at the threshold of choice with an unlimited
spectrum of experience stretching before me.
I bravely face the brokenness of my heart, mind,
and body, and through acceptance, darkness is
transmuted into awareness.
This is the process of transformation, alchemizing
shadow into pure gold.

ASCENSION (DETAIL)

(opposite)

GNOSIS
7"x9" acrylic & gold-leaf on panel, 2022

FATE
10"x12" acrylic & gold leaf on panel, 2022

"The past is exhausted from holding all your grievances, traumas, and personal history. The future is bored, holding onto all of your expectations and judgements of what 'should' be. Let go of the baggage, we don't need it where we're going."

— AUBREY MARCUS

THE CHOICE
20"x30" acrylic & gold leaf on panel, 2022

This is for the ones labelled and burned as witches;
for the ones raped and erased on their own indigenous land;
the ones forced to veil their faces; the ones sold into slavery;
the ones robbed of their childhood.
It is for the ones stripped of their language, music, and dance;
the ones who have been persecuted for their differences;
the ones scarred by wars that were not theirs;
the ones living in the shadow of abuse.
For those whose body autonomy has been stolen,
whose voices have been muted.
For the ones whose connection to the earth has been severed;
for the blood that has been spilled
and the countless names that we will never know.

This is a mirror to the warrior spirit within us all:
fierce, resilient, graceful, and true.
We are stepping out of our victim stories
and into our reclamation of personal and collective power, agency, and co-creativity.

May we stand strong in our knowing,
claiming our birthright of protest and defiance when essential,
while embodying the wisdom of our learned experience.
May we remember our power to make change where needed and possible,
while accepting and surrendering to the ebb and flow
of divine unfolding and growth.

May our eyes be focused, our minds clear, our boundaries healthy,
and our hearts steadfastly open.

WARRIOR
24"x30" acrylic & gold leaf on panel, 2023

AutumnSkye 2022

(opposite)

DAUGHTER OF THE SUN
16"x20" acrylic & gold leaf on panel, 2022

INNOCENCE
12"x16" acrylic & gold leaf on panel, 2020

Life is full of paradox...
the in-breath and the out-breath of existence,
the dance of duality,
the multifaceted spectrum of greys within
the self-perpetuating myth of black and white.

We are but a tiny speck,
scurrying around on a tiny speck, which is ceaselessly hurtling through space
in an eternal celestial dance.
Our lives are trivial and insignificant.
We are minuscule and inconsequential in the vast scale of the cosmos.

And yet, simultaneously, we are Divinity incarnate.
We are each unique facets of God, the universe embodied in human form.
Individually and collectively we are cultivating a new paradigm of cosmic evolution.
Every person, every mind and heart is vital and unfathomably meaningful to the whole.

Both of these truths coexist in perpetual ebb and flow.
In that eternally spiralling Yin Yang of complexity, contrast, and nuance
we can find sanctuary within the great mystery.

Breathe in, and breathe out.
Full and empty and full again.
Life, death, rebirth.
Yearning and grateful.
Ephemeral and eternal.

PARADOX
12"x14" acrylic & gold leaf on panel, 2022

THE ALLEGORY OF TIME
8"x10" acrylic & gold leaf on canvas, 2022

(opposite)
THE PHILOSOPHER
16"x20" acrylic & gold leaf on canvas, 2023

(opposite)
CORONATION
12"x16" acrylic & gold leaf on panel, 2020

IMAGINATION
13"x15" acrylic & gold leaf on panel, 2021

This is a time for fierce love...
A resilient love that can bridge the chasm of disconnection and weather the storm of uncertainty.
A love that meets fear with unyielding courage, heals division with humble acceptance,
and comforts suffering with tenderness. A love that is relentlessly compassionate to ourselves and others
as we navigate this tumultuous journey. Burn steady, dear heart, shine bright in the darkness.

(opposite)

THE ALCHEMY OF US
11"x14" acrylic & gold leaf on panel, 2020

FIERCE LOVE
30"x40" acrylic & gold leaf on panel, 2019

We honour the children who follow after us. We steward life with care and reverence, nurturing and respecting the balance of nature so that all may thrive in harmony. Our legacy is love. May future generations live and flourish on this sacred Earth. We celebrate the vitality of new life, the unique spark of each spirit, and the gifts that they carry to share with the world. In their reflection, may we remember our hope, innocence, curiosity, and playfulness.

We honour the elders who came before us. We celebrate the carriers of story, the ancestors of our bones and breath, and the weavers of time. We bow in gratitude for their generosity of wisdom, their enduring presence, and their benevolent magic. We are remembering our interconnectedness with the trees, the mountains, the water, and the wind.

Let us gather up the children and return to the feet of the ancient ones.

(opposite)

RESILIENCE
12"x16" acrylic & gold leaf on panel, 2017

FORGOTTEN ELDERS
16"x20" acrylic & gold leaf on panel, 2020

AXIOM
14"x20" acrylic & gold leaf on panel, 2017

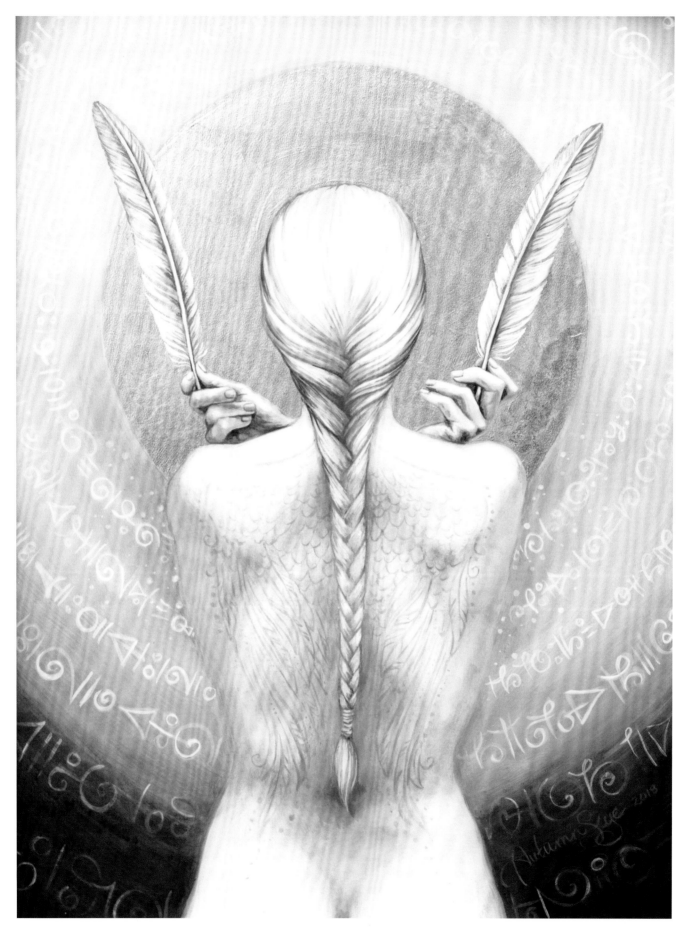

THE THEORY OF FLIGHT
16"x20" acrylic & gold leaf on panel, 2018

NOBLE TRUTH
8"x10" acrylic on panel, 2022

PROTECTION
12"x16" acrylic & gold leaf on panel, 2022

ASCENSION
12"x16" acrylic & gold leaf on panel, 2020

(opposite)
SERAPHIM
12"x16" acrylic & gold leaf on panel, 2020

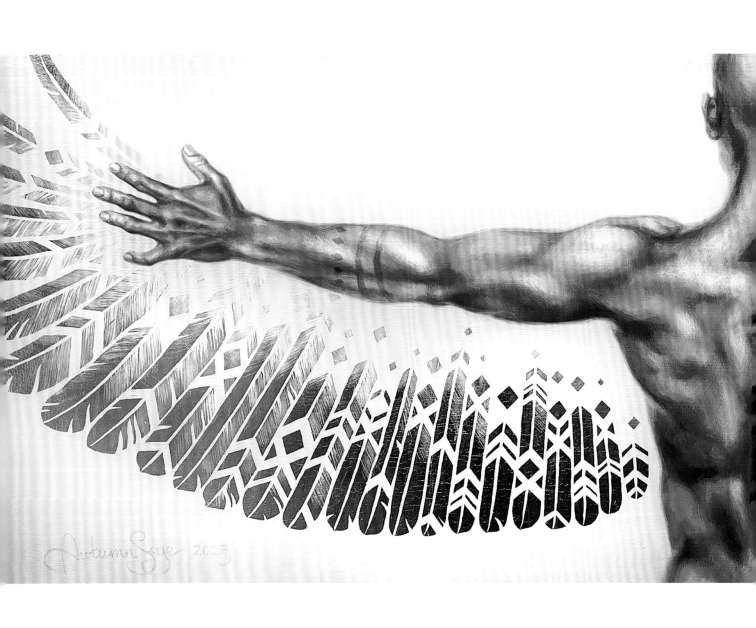

BECOMING
36"x12" acrylic & gold leaf on canvas, 2023

I'm not telling you it's going to be easy -
I'm telling you it's going to be worth it.

— Art Williams

Thank you for joining me
on this journey of
Art & Soul

♥

Autumn Skye

Photo by Adam Ziorio

AUTUMN SKYE

Autumn Skye lives, breathes, and dreams art, and has done so since she was old enough to hold a pencil and reach for a piece of paper. Her childhood and early adult years were spent travelling the landscapes of both her wild Canadian backyard and distant international shores. Through her wanderlust, she developed a deep reverence for the beauty of nature and the diversity of humanity, and continuously endeavours to translate this inspiration through her work.

As a self-taught artist, she is forever a student of the intuitively creative process. Autumn Skye's style weaves together refined realism, iconic imagery, archetypical symbolism, and spiritual principles. She's inspired by the magnificence of this incredible planet, the potency of these extraordinary times, and the mysteries of the cosmos. Through her work, she seeks to honour the resiliency of the human spirit and the intricate connections between all facets of life.

Autumn Skye exhibits and teaches worldwide, and otherwise thrives and paints in the beautiful temperate-rainforest of coastal British Columbia, Canada. Considering herself immensely blessed to do what feeds her soul, she strives to support others through creative empowerment, the gift of beauty, and the perpetuation of inspiration.

Photo by Sydney Woodward

GRATITUDE

Thank you, Mama, for your patience, playful, and skilful editing efforts.
Your ruthless and compassionate feedback has helped make this book what it is.
That goes for my paintings and the fun and challenging game of titling as well.
I am profoundly and eternally grateful for your unwavering support,
since I first picked up a pencil as a young child.

Thank you, Neo, for your amazing and thoughtful perspective and perception.
I am so grateful for your loving and enthusiastic cheerleading, your honest
and generous critiques, and your wholehearted belief in my creative path.

Thank you to my teachers, my students, my family, and my beloved brothers
and sisters who inspire me with their stories and grace.

Thank YOU, the one holding this book. Thank you for your enduring support,
your inspiring and insightful reflections, and for your generous words of encouragement.
I am deeply honoured that you bring these paintings into your world,
and am grateful that you join me on this incredible and
mysterious journey of art, imagination, and spirit.

Copyright © 2024 Autumn Skye
www.AutumnSkyeArt.com

All rights reserved.
Other than for personal use, no part of this book may be reproduced
in any way, in whole or part, without the written consent of the
copyright holder or publisher. The views and opinions expressed by the author
both within and outside of this publication do not necessarily reflect
the views of the publisher.

Published by Blue Angel Publishing®
10 Trafford Court, Wheelers Hill
Victoria, Australia 3150
Email: info@blueangelonline.com
Website: www.blueangelonline.com

Unless otherwise noted, all text by Autumn Skye.

Layout Designer: Kelly Jewell

Edited by Peter Loupelis

Blue Angel is a registered trademark of Blue Angel Gallery Pty Ltd.

ISBN: 978-1-922574-15-2